Against
the Light

essential translations series 9

Canada Council Conseil des Arts
for the Arts du Canada

ONTARIO ARTS COUNCIL
CONSEIL DES ARTS DE L'ONTARIO

50 YEARS OF ONTARIO GOVERNMENT SUPPORT OF THE ARTS
50 ANS DE SOUTIEN DU GOUVERNEMENT DE L'ONTARIO AUX ARTS

Guernica Editions Inc. acknowledges the support of
the Canada Council for the Arts and the Ontario Arts Council.
The Ontario Arts Council is an agency of the Government of Ontario. We
acknowledge the financial support of the Government of Canada through
the Canada Book Fund (CBF) for our publishing activities.

Against the Light

Tiziano Broggiato

Translated from the Italian
by Patricia Hanley and Maria Laura Mosco

An Italian-English Bilingual Edition

GUERNICA

TORONTO – BUFFALO – BERKELEY – LANCASTER (U.K.) 2012

Copyright © 2001, Tiziano Broggiato and Marsilio Editori
Original title: *Parca lux*
Translation Copyright © 2012, Patricia Hanley, Maria Laura
Mosco and Guernica Editions Inc.

Michael Mirolla, editor
Guernica Editions Inc.
P.O. Box 117, Station P, Toronto (ON), Canada M5S 2S6
2250 Military Road, Tonawanda, N.Y. 14150-6000 U.S.A.

Distributors:
University of Toronto Press Distribution,
5201 Dufferin Street, Toronto (ON), Canada M3H 5T8
Gazelle Book Services, White Cross Mills, High Town,
Lancaster LA1 4XS U.K.
Small Press Distribution, 1341 Seventh St., Berkeley, CA
94710-1409 U.S.A.

First edition.
Printed in Canada.

Legal Deposit – Third Quarter

Library of Congress Catalog Card Number: 2012941658

Library and Archives Canada Cataloguing in Publication

Broggiato, Tiziano
Against the light / Tiziano Broggiato ; Patricia Hanley, Maria
Laura Mosco, translator. (Essential translations series ; 9)
Translation of: Parca lux.
Issued also in electronic format.
Poems in Italian and English.

ISBN 978-1-55071-663-4

I. Hanley, Patricia II. Mosco, Maria Laura III. Title.
IV. Series: Essential translations series (Toronto, Ont.) ;9.

PQ4862.R5855A52 2012   851'.914   C2012-904229-3

Contents

Preface

This translation of a nearly complete selection from Tiziano Broggiato's fourth, and prize winning volume, *Parca lux*, came about almost by chance when, in 2002, it was discovered in Florence in a bookstore on a table laden with contemporary Italian poetry. It was another year before we, the translators, learned that it had won Italy's prestigious Montale prize in that same year, 2002. Meanwhile, we had been granted the authority to be its sole translators into English. One hesitates to call it fate after an extraordinary decade of living closely with this remarkable work but it may be worth noting that *Parcae* means "the fates" in Latin: *Parca*, therefore, is a "goddess of fate."

Parca lux, the beacon which illumines even as it fades, and now given the title, *Against the Light*, begins with "Flight's Elegy," a poem which, in its structure and measured pace, speaks with near-biblical authority and illustrates the full power of Broggiato's poetic imagination. In the haunted voices of father and son there is, in the words of one Italian critic, Giovanni Salviati, an intense, mysterious rendering of the modern state of disorientation [*una intensa, misteriosa traduzione dello spaesamento moderno*]. Here are the profoundly moving voices of exile, loss and spiritual abandonment.

Poems which follow raise the question of influence, of those poets, past and present, who hover as ghosts, often without leaving any discernible traces. Broggiato has been schooled in the classical poets. Of Italy's modern writers: Montale, Sereni and Luzi. Much younger, and therefore less well known to the English reader, are Milo de Angelis and Roberto Mussapi. The final lines in the last poem are an evocation, and disturbing reminder, of their presence:

> *(Sometimes*
>   *in sleep*
> *I hear you cry out*
> *to the whirlpools of the Adriatic:*
> *each with the name*
> *of a poet you used to quote.*
> *The tremor that wakes you*
> *as it crashes among these ghosts*
> *is the last barrier*
> *separating your life from theirs.)*

Of the twentieth century's European poets, the one who truly haunts this work and is central to some of its most starkly disturbing and beautiful poems is Paul Celan, the latter half of the twentieth century's greatest poet in the German language and, for some, indisputably its greatest. For Broggiato, he is one of the rarest, most influential and venerated poets of that century [... *uno dei rarissimi poeti ... è uno dei poeti più influenti e venerati del '900*]. He is here in spirit, a revenant of the Shoah, with a power that can threaten to overpower into a silence deeply and terribly rooted in that reality, from which the light of his poetry emerged. In the *Parca Lux* grouping of poems are these last lines from "Celan's Affliction":

> *In a while*
> *strange identical moths will come*

hurled into this womb of savagery
towards the end of their brief journeying:

towards that final light
                    when
born into a confusion of charred wings
they'll rise immutable in the blazing sky
of another
                    ravaged Warsaw.

The poem, "May 12th," marks the date of Paul Celan's burial in Paris, following his suicide in 1970.

Against the Light is suffused with memory's evocations of place and time which express their deep rootedness in Italy. There are the poems of childhood's dream at Peschiera del Garda, of poignant returns, of luminous joy within the dark pain of existence. One or two can be held in a single breath; others take the reader to the very edge of palpable silence. This is the work of a mature poet and a poetry of remarkable, transcendent beauty. It seems fitting to give the last word to Mario Luzi, Italy's revered poet who died at the age of 90, in 2005:

> "What makes Broggiato's poetry emblematic and figurative is its internal development which creates flashes of lightning both revelatory and full of warning. The poems are marked by a forceful beauty, exciting in the reader an urgency parallel to that of the writer." [*Ciò che rende emblematica e sintomatica la poesia di Broggiato è quel processo intestino che essa provoca generando lampi eloquenti e ammonitori. Sono versi, questi, stigmi di energica bellezza che servono ad eccitare il rovello del lettore in parallelo con quello dello scrittore.*]

Patricia Hanley

Elogio della fuga

——

Flight's Elegy

Elogio della fuga

– Dimmi padre da chi stiamo fuggendo
e per quale demone abbiamo attraversato
interminabili campi d'orzo
e costeggiato dirupi senza mai fermarci.
I sandali mi hanno piagato i piedi
e ora i voli radenti dei gracchi
annunciano la notte. Sostiamo
in questo campo di pervinche a riposare.
Potremo rifocillarci. E riflettere.
Da ore abbiamo perduto di vista
le luci degli ultimi fuochi
e non si odono più nemmeno
i belati delle greggi.
Fermiamoci prima che il buio imminente
celi la pista e ci faccia precipitare – .

– Non odi allora le voci dietro di noi
che danno i brividi?
Esse si mantengono a distanza costante
per non insospettirci
ma le odo ugualmente
e dal loro tono so che
sono irritate perché abbiamo rallentato
il passo. Ma se oseremo fermarci
la loro ira ci raggiungerà
annebbiandoci la vista
e facendoci dividere e disperdere
per sempre – .

Flight's Elegy

– Father, tell me who we are running from.
What demons have made us cross
these interminable fields of barley
and keep to the cliff edge
without ever stopping. My sandals
have blistered my feet and now
ravens are flying close by
announcing nightfall. Let's stay here
and rest in this field of flowers.
We'll catch our breath and reflect.
By now we've lost
the light from the last fires
and can no longer hear the sheep bleating.
Let's stop before the coming darkness
makes us lose our way and fall headlong –.

– Don't you hear the voices behind us then –
voices that make me tremble?
They keep their distance
so we won't suspect anything
but I hear them nevertheless
and from their tone I know
they're angry because we've
slowed down. But if we dare stop
their anger will overtake us
it will muddle us; we'll be forced
to separate and so
be lost to each other forever –.

– Sono forse sterpi spazzate dal vento
                              padre
e non voci.
Nessuno è irato con noi.
Le nostre genti vivono in pace
e vi rispettano. Ogni tribù dei dintorni
vi riconosce sapienza e vi
affida le sentenze per le cause
più importanti.
Ritorniamo ai tappeti e alle maioliche
della nostra casa.
Pensate a mia madre
e alle mie sorelle che si staranno
aggirando di casa in casa
chiedendo nostre notizie – .

– Per noi mai più
potrà esserci ritorno.
Ciò che abbiamo lasciato
è ormai sprofondato nel flagello
di cenere e ossa da me
provocato accettando lo scambio – .

– Di quale scambio parlate
                         padre?
Svelatemi il vostro segreto – .

– È il timore di perderti
                         figlio mio
di saperti rapito dalle voci
che mi inquieta.
Sono venute all'alba
per annunciarmi di averti scelto
come loro prossimo compagno di viaggio.
E ti volevano subito
senza ritardi né rinvii.

– Perhaps it's the wind in the bare branches

                       father

and not voices.
No one is angry with us.
Our people live in peace
and they respect you. All the tribes around
know of your wisdom and trust
your judgment in everything
that matters most.
Let's go back to the carpets and majolica
of our home.
Think of my mother
and sisters who must be wandering
from house to house asking
for news of us –.

– For us
return is no longer possible.
By now whatever we have left is buried
beneath the scourge of bones
and ashes that I provoked
by accepting the exchange –.

– What exchange are you talking about

                      father?

Do tell me your secret –.

– It's my fear of losing you

                    my son

of knowing your enchantment with their voices
that unsettles me.
They came at dawn
to let me know they had chosen you
as their next companion for the voyage.
They wanted you immediately
without delay or postponement.

Ti ho difeso con disperazione.
Ho offerto stagno e ambra
le nostre ricchezze ...
... me stesso al posto tuo
ma loro hanno rifiutato di ascoltarmi.
Ho implorato il tempo

almeno

per prepararmi...
Solo allora hanno parlato:
"Nulla ti è dovuto
ma per la tua nota saggezza
ti concediamo una prova" – .

Così ...
(Sotto mentite spoglie
alla fine del pasto
si alzò la Cananea
e indicando le tre donne
sedute intorno al fuoco
le accusò di non aver saputo
nemmeno attendere la notte
per appartarsi dagli altri.

– Non hanno pace tra noi.
Non usano lo stesso unguento
con cui curiamo le nostre ferite.
Ascoltano solo il livore
che le perseguita e sono qui
per diffonderne il contagio.
Guardatele: anche la forma
dei loro occhi è cambiata:
col tempo sono diventate aguzze
perfino le lamine sbalzate

I was desperate to protect you.
I offered tin and amber
our riches ...
... myself in your place
but they refused to listen to me.
I begged for time

                    at least

to prepare myself ...
At this point they said:
"Nothing is owed you
but in view of your renowned wisdom
we grant you one single trial" –.

                    So ...
                    (Using a false name
                    the Canaanite woman rose
                    at the end of the meal
                    and pointing to the three women
                    seated around the fire

                    accused them of not even being able
                    to wait for nightfall
                    to be separated from the others.

                    – They are not at peace with us.
                    They don't treat their wounds
                    with the same ointments we use.
                    All they listen to is the spite
                    that trails after them; they're here
                    to spread their contagion.
                    Look at them: even the expression
                    in their eyes has changed:
                    it has become more intense
                    and they're constantly

delle loro ciglia.
È per questo loro silenzio colpevole
e per l'approssimarsi della notte in cui
tutti dovremo vegliare
per la nostra salvezza
che vi chiedo di consegnarmele –).

– Mia madre. Le mie sorelle! –

(Le donne
                    impaurite
si strinsero tra loro.

– Purché non ci trafigga lei stessa
nel sonno ...

– Finché la memoria non sarà
troppo lontana ...

Ma un anziano del popolo
conoscendo le origini dell'impostura
si rivolse a me per designare
il loro destino: alzò con una sola mano
il bimbo che teneva
stretto fra le ginocchia
e mostrandolo alle genti del campo
mi costrinse a pronunciarmi.

– Parla Sidonio. Decidi che
sia sacrificato questo fanciullo
per donare la salvezza alle donne
o che siano loro
consegnate per prime
alle ragioni della Cananea –).

frowning as well.
Because of this guilty silence of theirs
and the approach of night
when everyone must be vigilant
for our safety's sake
I ask you to hand them over to me –).

– My mother. My sisters! –

(The terrified women
                                        clung
to each other.

– As long as she doesn't stab us
in our sleep …

– As long as remembrance isn't
too far off …

But an elder of the people
knowing the source of the imposture
turned towards me to indicate
their fate: with one hand
he lifted the infant he was holding
firmly between his knees
and showing him to the people of the camp
forced me to speak up.

– Speak Sidonio. Decide whether
this child is to be sacrificed
in order to save the women
or if they are to be handed over
to the Canaanite, first and foremost
for the reasons she has given –).

Lo sgomento mi invase
impedendomi di parlare e perfino
di alzarmi.
Anche se in cuor mio la scelta
era già avvenuta
i loro occhi imploranti
colmi d'innocente certezza
mi bloccarano.
Ma tu mi devi capire:
per ognuna di loro
ancora una speranza
un po' più di tempo per te ...

– Ora finalmente conosco il senso della fuga.
Volevate allontanarmi dalle voci
sacrificando al mio posto mia madre
e le mie sorelle.
Come avete potuto
come riuscirete a sopravvivere al rimorso?
Vi compatisco padre mio:
avete solo ritardato il mio momento
devastando la nostra famiglia.
Se loro hanno scelto me
nessuno scambio o fuga riuscirà
a farle desistere da ciò che già
è stato scritto – .

– Non ancora.
Appena questo vento impetuoso si placherà
riprenderemo il cammino.
Le tenebre ci saranno propizie
per eludere la loro sorveglianza.
Ci muoveremo con circospezione.
Ascolta anche tu attentamente:
non si ode più il loro brusio dietro di noi.
Forse avranno ceduto alla stanchezza

I was stricken
unable to speak, not even
able to rise.
Even if in my heart
I had already made my choice
their imploring eyes
full of innocent trust
paralysed me.
But you must understand me:
for each one of them
there was yet one hope
a little more time for you ...

– Now I finally understand the meaning of our flight.
You wanted to take me far away from the voices
sacrificing my mother and sisters
instead of me.
How could you –
how will you survive your remorse?
My father, I pity you:
You've only delayed my moment
that completes the devastation of our family.
If they have chosen me
no exchange or flight
will keep them from
what has already been written –.

– Not yet.
As soon as this terrible wind dies down
we'll continue walking.
The dark will give us the advantage
in avoiding their watch.
We'll move cautiously.
Listen carefully:
we no longer hear their muttering behind us.
Maybe they have given up in exhaustion

perdendoci di vista ...

– Padre
            tornate in voi.
Non vi rendete dunque conto?
Non udite più le voci
perché ci hanno già raggiunto
e oltrepassato.
Erano il vento di poco fa.
Noi non siamo più quelli di prima.
Il destino alla fine si è compiuto.
Siamo entrambi diventati anime.
Solo anime –.

and have lost sight of us ...

– Father,
            stop this.
Haven't you realized?
You don't hear the voices
because they've already caught up with us
and have gone beyond.
They were the wind you heard awhile ago.
We are no longer what we were before.
It has come to pass.
We have become spirits, both of us.
Only spirits –.

Parca lux

—

Parca Lux

Il contagio di Celan

I treni della notte
sono secchi schiocchi di frusta
sulle palpebre dei bambini
allineati a Czernowitz.

Si diffonde
            nei vagoni piombati
la loro nenia ininterrotta:
forse sanno o hanno intuito
l'avvicendarsi dei custodi.

Fra poco
identiche straordinarie falene
verranno spinte nel ventre della fiera
verso la loro corsa più breve:

verso la definitiva luce
                        quando
mutate in smarrite ali nere
saliranno per sempre nel cielo più caldo
di un'altra
            devastata Varsavia.

Celan's Affliction

The night trains
are quick cracks of the whip
on the eyelids of the children
lined up at Czernowitz.

Like ether spreading
                    through the leaded cars
their voices' ceaseless wailing:
perhaps they know or have sensed
the routine passing of the guards.

In a while
strange identical moths will come
hurled into this womb of savagery
towards the end of their brief journeying:

towards that final light
                    when
born into a confusion of charred wings
they'll rise immutable in the blazing sky
of another
                    ravaged Warsaw.

Voce
      dispersa
            nel deserto più deserto
nel vasto nulla di questo secolo nebbioso

e poi muta
nella perpetrazione della Shoah
e lungo il tragitto che conduce
alle porte segnate col gesso.

Al di là
      un cielo traslucido:
il taglio netto degli anni
sceso con te nell'oblio.

A voice
      cast upon
                wastelands more desolate
in the void of this shadowed century

then the silence
in the perpetration of Shoah
along a passage that leads
to the doorways signed with chalk.

Beyond
      a transparent sky:
the lucid clearing away of years
descended with you into oblivion.

12 Maggio

Ha zigomi alti
                   quasi tartari
e uno sguardo svagato
l'angelo che riposa laggiù
nel campo di Bertesina.
Ci intendevamo bene lui ed io
ci intendiamo ancora:
dagli opposti oblò ci scambiamo
discreti favori e notizie
a giorni alterni.

È quasi tutto come prima.

Solo talvolta
mi concedo di rimproverarlo
per l'improvviso sonno
e quella mano inerte
                        aperta
che rivelò il buio inaudito
dietro la sua testa.

May 12th

His high cheekbones
                    almost a Tartar's
his gaze, absentminded –
the angel resting down below
in the Bertesina court.
We've been on good terms, he and I
and still are:
we exchange news and tactful greetings
from our opposite portholes
every other day.

Everything is more or less as it was before.

Only sometimes
I allow myself to reproach him
for suddenly falling asleep
and for that lifeless, open
                              hand
that revealed the unheard darkness
behind his head.

Visita a Treblinka

In quale limbo
o luogo di temporanea dimora
attesero il suono dei passi
e il ringhiare dei cani.

Alla luce cattiva del giorno
nessuno riconobbe i loro volti
mentre venivano condotti al campo
in cui da ogni pietra alzata
sarebbe scaturita per sempre
una marea di schiume rosse.

Ora
        nella piana degli spiriti attoniti
nel silenzio livido dei loro dormitori
pare solo sospeso il richiamo
dei giocolieri con le bolle di sapone:

l'odore dei fuochi è rimasto
e non si è arrestato nemmeno
al di là del filo spinato
il tintinnio che il vento cadenza ancora
attraversando la cremagliera
di quella stessa giostra abbandonata.

15 Gennaio 1998

Visit to Treblinka

In what way station
or makeshift enclosure
did they wait for the tramp of feet
and the snarl of dogs.

In the brutal light of day
their faces were indistinguishable
as they were led into the camp
where for all of future time
from every raised stone
would issue a tide of blood-red foam.

Now
        in the open field of stricken ghosts
in the bruised silence of their dormitories
as if suspended there, the shout
of jugglers with their bubbles of soap:

the odour of fires remains
even a jangled sound persists
beyond the barbed wires
as the wind in passing beats
on the cog-wheel
of that same abandoned merry-go-round.

January 15, 1998

Lì
    nel livore della soglia
tra alba e alba
lo sgomento della repentina resa.

Del tuo pianto senza soluzione.

There
        at the hostile threshold
between dawn and dawn
the anguish of your sudden surrender.

Your irresolvable tears.

Nulla resta della tua fuga:
né l'ustione del legno
                              né l'ira
verso la mano dei tuoi giustizieri.
Era stata la cieca
                    a predire
a metà del ponte
la tua esitazione:
di qua mille porte attendevano
di essere aperte dalla tua chiave
di là altrettante ombre da inseguire.

Sei stato visto aprirti un varco nel parapetto
con un solo gesto della mano
e scendere in acqua
quasi senza sollevare spruzzi.

Per il mio ansante rincorrerti
nel momento della caduta
fammi incrociare il tuo remo.
All'ora
        ti prego
non lasciarmi avanzare a vista.

Nothing is left of your flight
not the burning wood
                              not the anger
against the hand of your executioners.
Blind fate
                    foretold
your hesitation
halfway across the bridge
here – a thousand doors were waiting
to be opened with your key
there – as many ghosts compelling you to follow.

On that parapet they saw you find your way
with a single wave of your hand –
your descent into the water
barely making a ripple.

In my breathless effort to pursue you
at the moment of your fall
let your oar guide me across.
At the last
                    I beg of you
let me reach beyond my sight.

È lo stesso tempo in bilico
di alarmi e preghiere
che privò altri padri
della necessaria purificazione
quello che adesso ci coglie
con la supplica negli occhi
affinché anche in queste albe
sempre più tardive
la dissolvenza della profezia
non sia così imminente.

Allora le pattinatrici jugoslave
scendevano la Drina gelata
per immolarsi
nel nome breve dei vivi
sulle grate di un fiume
dai fianchi per sempre straziati.

Ora
     l'estrema contesa dei loro figli
su chi per primo li designò
persecutori o martiri
nella medesima rosa
è solo un mormorio soffocato
oltre una porta ben chiusa.

«Nessuno vedrà per due volte
la luce dell'angelo».

«Nessun superstite rimarrà
dopo il ritiro delle acque».

It is the same time of uncertainty
of warnings and prayers
that deprived other forebears
of the necessary purification –
a time that seizes hold here
with eyes of entreaty
that the fading of prophecy
not be that imminent
even in these dawns
always so much slower to arrive.

Then, the women skaters of Yugoslavia
as a sacrifice
in the fleeting name of the living
went down to the frozen Drina
onto the iron grid of the river
whose banks are strife-torn forever.

Now
        the greatest dispute among their children
about who first appointed them
persecutors or martyrs
in the self-same circle
is just a stifled murmur
beyond a sealed door.

"No one will see the light
of the angel twice."

"No one will survive
after the flood waters recede."

Umbra sine spe

Tra le pietre sgretolate
della tua casa di Romania
solo il pianto di Rachele
è rimasto lo stesso di quando
le annunciasti che il suo doriforo
prediletto avrebbe sepolto
ogni esatta memoria
per perseguire solo il verbo
nella sua folle sublimazione.

Ma la peste non concede tregue
e da quel momento latte e acqua
smisero di sgorgare dalle fessure
di tutte le tue dimore
né alcun Giano guardò più
le tue porte soffocando per te
il fragore degli spari
in avvicinamento.

– Non confessare
non manifestare il tuo smarrimento
alle dolenti senza labbra –
fu ancora la sua preghiera
quando la luce
che si alzava dai tuoi occhi
giunse a distinguere appena
la fiamma e la verbena
tra le cui dita avevi un tempo
conosciuto la pace

Umbra Sine Spe

Among the shattered ruins
of your Romanian home
only Rachel's weeping
remains the same as the time
when you announced to her
that the chosen guard would bury
every faithful memory
intent alone
upon the word's mad exaltation.

But the plague grants no reprieve
and from that moment milk and water
ceased to flow from the cracks
of all your dwellings
nor did any Janus keep further watch
at your door
to stifle the din
of approaching rifle fire.

– Don't confess
don't show your loss
to those who are silent –
it was still her prayer
when the light
that rose from your eyes came
barely to discern
the fire and the verbena –
fingers that once
had let you find peace –

(e già sapevi che nella tua grotta
si aggiravano le fiere
che avrebbero instillato i loro spasmi
nei tuoi sonni).

Oh parca lux
se l'urgenza della voce chiede davvero
che attorno il mondo si svuoti
perché non ti rivelasti almeno
per ritardare quell'ultimo istante
sul parapetto del ponte Mirabeau?

(you already knew beasts
were at large in your cave
and would enter your dreams
with their convulsions).

Oh parca lux
if the urgency of your voice truly insists
that our world be left empty
why didn't you reveal yourself at least
to delay that last moment
on the parapet of the pont Mirabeau?

Finestre

—

The View Beyond

Finestra di grattacielo

Nel silenzio del corridoio
ho udito lo sfilarsi della faretra
e il soffio che precede il colpo
del suo richiamo nel buio sottostante.

Poi
     affacciato dal quarantesimo piano
l'ho sentito nettamente oscillare
questo immenso arco
impugnato da mano di ciclope
intento a tenderne il nervo
mentre io
         tra pupilla e mirino
ne attendo l'imminente sibilo
che mi scaglierà lontanissimo
in un tragitto più vicino al cielo
oltre lo sterminato orizzonte di dita tese

verso un'ignara preda
             tra Gerico e Sidone.

Window of a Skyscraper

In the silence of the corridor
I heard the arrow taken from its quiver
and just before the strike
an echo murmured in the dark below.

Then
        leaning from the fortieth floor
I clearly felt
this huge bow's oscillation
gripped in a cyclopean hand
intent on bending it
while I
        between the pupil and the line of sight
wait for the imminent hissing
that will hurl me far on its skyward path
across the vast horizon of fingers tensed

against an unsuspecting prey
        between Jericho and Sidon.

Centro di salute mentale

Li vedo dalla mia finestra
nel giardinetto sottostante
seduti in cerchio come
in un consiglio di capi indiani
dove nessuno parla oppure
sono le volute di fumo
dei loro calumet
a comunicare
lo stato di ognuno.

Qui
  al sicuro del fortino
dietro le attente guardie di confine
non smette un giorno di pulsarmi
nelle tempie il doloroso allarme
del colpo ricevuto di striscio.

Mental Health Centre

From my window I see them
in their little garden down below
sitting in a circle
like a tribal council
where no one speaks.
Instead the plumes of smoke
from their pipes
tell them
how everyone is.

Here
       in the safety of my fortress
no day goes by without
the pulsing in my temples
of a painful alarm over a glancing blow
behind that carefully guarded frontier.

Al di là dei vetri
nel quieto traffico serale
quanti fra quelli che ora
si stanno dirigendo
verso più ospitali silenzi
o vanno a consegnarsi
ad altri
                ordinati inferni
sapranno di avere già contratto
il morbo
o il contagio
che fra tre
                o sei mesi
o un anno li vedrà
inesorabilmente assorbiti
dalla gelida ragnatela
della dissoluzione?

Beyond these windows
in evening traffic's calm
how many of them
now heading
for friendlier silences
or about to give in
to other
            neat and tidy hells
will realize they've already contracted
the infectious disease
the contagion
that in three
            or six months
or a year
will see them inescapably
caught in the petrified web
of their own undoing?

Le terre riemerse

—

Resurgent Lands

Ritorno a Peschiera del Garda

Ho viaggiato da solo
verso l'estrema Tule
verso le acque increspate
dei miei primi dieci anni.
Dove sono ora i suoi galeoni
e le luci azzurre della sua freccia?
Non c'è più tempo per l'apnea
dietro la porta socchiusa:
tra vampe troppo brevi
nella gelida nebbia decembrina
mi fermerò
         tra poco
all'inizio del ponte di ferro
senza attraversarlo. Di là
sono sicuro
         c'è ancora una memoria:
il segreto del bimbo sognatore
che mai dovrà essere svelato.

Return to Peschiera del Garda

I travelled alone
towards Ultima Thule
towards the rippled waters
of my first ten years.
Where are its galleons now
the blue rays of its summit?
The time is past for breathlessness
behind the half-closed door:
in a blaze all too brief
in December's freezing mists
I will stop
            soon
at the threshold of the iron bridge
without crossing. From there
I am sure
            of yet another memory:
the secret of a dreaming child
never to be revealed.

Breve diario dalla terra riemersa

Un vento di troppe foglie
infiltra all'interno dell'auto
un odore acuto di cenere e neve.
È strana Brooklyn alle sei del mattino
con questo intenso mulinare
di manine tronche che permette
di intuire appena i suoi bastioni
la grossa gobba di animale
acquattato nel semibuio e aizzato
dai lucori dei precoci risvegli.

Dall'ultimo viale di alberi neri
ormai al sicuro verso Long Island
non avverto più i suoi gorgoglii
l'aspro alito delle sue viscere
e gli sterminati vapori
che ne preludono il necessario
inabissamento.

Qui
        dove i bassi palmeti
sono flessi dal rinforzo del vento
e il fragore delle onde ritma
il respiro mi rinviene chiaro
il monito dell'Arcangelo sull'estrema
cresta di Atlantide: «Questa terra
che nasconde ciò che si prese
nel castigo del buio perenne
riemergerà un'unica volta

Brief Diary from a Resurgent Land

Leaf-stirring gusts of wind
bring a sharp odour of ash and snow
straight into the car.
At six in the morning Brooklyn is eerie –
with this intense whir of stunted hands
it is just possible
to make out its ramparts
a large, hunched animal
crouched in the half-dark, goaded
by the lights from an awakening city.

Along the last avenue of black trees
by now heading safely towards Long Island
I no longer notice its rumblings
the sour breath of its entrails
and the endless fumes
that foreshadow its inevitable
sinking.

Here
          where palm groves
bend with the force of the wind
and each beating breath of thundering
waves clearly recalls me to the warning
of the Archangel on the outermost
ridge of Atlantis: "This land
punished by eternal darkness
that hides what it grasped for itself
will re-emerge one last time

per conoscere luci di albe così profonde
che solo gli occhi dei più forti
potranno sopportare».

Poi rallento
                    a Tulash Bay
per seguire sulla banchina i riti
del tuffatore che si appresta
a entrare nell'oceano
                            nudo
eppure indifferente al gelo
rappreso nella sua ipnotica incolumità
di angelo: mi colpisce il suo sorriso
estatico
            a occhi chiusi
mentre si tende in volo.
Un sorriso solo dei folli.

– It will snow! –
mi saluta il doganiere dal pontile
indicando l'arrivo della tempesta:
un sospeso grigio in cui appaiono
e scompaiono sagome di navi
e fendenti di gabbiani
che
        come mesti e vecchi dèi abdicanti
ripiegano sul molo trasalendo appena
per la presenza di noi
altri compagni di naufragio.

Da quaggiù
nel riverbero d'inchiostri e cere
la città irraggia lampi delle sue
chiuse rovine.
                    Nell'andarmene
il mattino seguente

to witness the radiance of dawns so profound
that only the eyes of the strong
will be able to endure it."

Then I slow down
                        at Tulash Bay
to observe the ritual of a diver on the wharf
who is preparing to enter
the ocean
            bared
but indifferent to the freezing cold
securely fixed in his hypnotic and angelic
state: I am struck by his ecstatic
smile
            eyes closed
while outstretched in flight.
A smile of the mad alone.

– It will snow! –
is the customs officer's greeting at the quay
pointing to the coming storm:
a grey heaviness
through which forms of ships appear and disappear
and seagulls strike out for the pier
like old
            and melancholy gods
who have abdicated –
startled just now by our presence:
more shipwrecked companions.

From here below
in the reverberation of inks and wax tablets
the city shines a brief light
over its hidden ruins.
                        Upon leaving
the following morning

ho visto scendervi la più bella neve
della mia vita

           ma sento che là
dove sono stato felice
dove ho molto immaginato
non dovrò mai tornare.

I saw the most beautiful snowfall
of my entire life

                but I know that
where I had been happy
where so much had been imagined
there I need never return.

Anima corallii

—

Anima Corallii

Così
          poco oltre il confine
anche la terza sentinella si è assopita.
Chi doveva vegliare con me
il veloce viaggio in autostrada
con confessioni complici
e inaspettati smarrimenti
si è infine arreso alla stanchezza.
Ora sono solo alla guida dell'auto
e ad arginare la resina dei ricordi
che cola sulle palpebre sfumando i nomi
delle uscite per città che non conosco.

          (Riodo i nostri bisbiglii
          nel freddo refettorio saveriano
          le nostre risa smorzate
          dal richiamo ieratico del prefetto).

Neppure l'improvviso scoppio
del colpo solo che ci sfiora il fianco
scomparendo poi davanti
nel buio dell'una di notte
turba il sonno dei miei compagni.
Sarà per antica fiducia nel postiglione?
O per la quieta sortita fuori casa?

          (Uno
                    per rappresaglia etica
          per esemplare formazione
          sarebbe uscito subito
                              senza cena
          dal luogo della comunione).
Un volontario

So
      a little beyond the border
the third watch had also dozed off –
the one who was supposed to join me
in keeping an eye on our highway speed.
With our accomplices' confessions
and unexpected wrong turns
he finally gave in to exhaustion.
Now I am alone at the wheel
holding back the resin's seep of memories
on my eyelids that blurs the names of exits
for cities I don't know.

                  (I hear our whispers again
                  in the cold St. Francis Xavier refectory
                  our muffled laughter
                  at the solemn rebuke of the prefect).

Not even the sudden bang of a side-
swiping then the disappearance ahead
in the dark at one in the morning
disturbs the sleep of my companions.
Could it be the ancient trust in the postilion?
Or the relaxation of just having left home?

                  (One
                        as an ethical reprisal
                  to set a good example
                  would have left the communal hall
                                          immediately
                  without dinner).
One volunteer
                  a reliable decoy

una fidata esca cui affidare
ora come allora
il compito della traversata.

(Scendere di nascosto la scala proibita
per portare fette di pane e cubetti di
marmellata
all'impavido achilleo
all'unico eroe considerato).

Ma io
scudiero o garzone
per quanto tempo ancora
i troverò a ringraziare questi dormienti
questi ipnotici profeti accondiscendenti
solo per essersi affidati
allora e ancora
alla mia estenuata devozione?

entrusted now, as then
with the tasks of the trip.

>   (To sneak down the prohibited stairway
>   taking bread and marmelade
>   to one of achillean bravery
>   the only worthy hero).

But
        for how long
shall I find myself
as equerry or servant boy
thanking these slumberers
these agreeable, hypnotic prophets
                                        then and yet again
just to keep them faithful
to my burnt-out devotion?

Crisalide

Uscito in fretta
                    fuggito
dai capogiri della camera
dall'orrendo gorgoglio di canne
ostruite
          di lui
che più non copre
nemmeno per pudicizia
le bende sulla gola

dai suoi occhi sgranati
con cui sembra voler divorare
le sembianze di tutti i presenti
(«Dio
          deve per forza andare così?»
lo udii farfugliare
nella fluttuante preanestesia).
Via dunque
                    lontano
dal gorgo implacabile.

Da quell'ultimo suo disperato
comunicare a gesti.

Chrysalis

I rush away
            flee
from the vertigo of the room
from the horror of his gurgling
blocked tubes
and the bandage that no longer
covers his throat
                 not even
for modesty's sake

from his wide-eyed stare
which seems to want to devour
everyone there
("God
         must it be like this?"
I heard babbled
in the flux of preanesthesia).
Away
      however far
from the unappeasable whirlpool.

From that last desperate sign.

L'uccello marino
che sul tetto della cappella
sfida impavido l'arrivo della tempesta
per poi fuggire goffamente
al solo suono di una voce
è l'esatto mio opposto

                      penso
che giro col sorriso
e un'ascia pronta
                  dietro le spalle.

The sea bird
on the roof of the chapel
that fearlessly braves the approaching storm
then flies away awkwardly
at the mere sound of a voice
                              I consider
my exact opposite.
I, who have a ready smile
and an axe handy
                    behind my back.

Precluse ogni memoria
il tacito armistizio:
«Mai più complici.
Mai più così vicini».

Eppure anche oggi
                    rincontrandoti
sarebbe sufficiente un giro d'occhi
uno scarto del tuo passo
colto nell'ombra della parete di fronte
per dare eternità all'acrobazia
di tutte le nostre riverberazioni.

The silent truce
forbade all memory.
"Never again complicit.
Never again so close."

Yet even today
                    meeting you again
that glance, that sudden, surprised side-
step in the shade of the wall opposite
would be enough to make all our
acrobatics echo forever.

Il portale scorto a malapena
tra calcinacci e impalcature
lasciati alle liane dell'incuria.
Un orto degli ulivi scovato
dal tuo bisogno di ascoltare
e ora attraversato a mani giunte
e con il passo breve del confidente
verso la voltina miracolosa.

Con un filo di perle nel tono
del rossetto – per rispetto – ti giustifichi –
della sacra dimora – accompagni
in tua vece la mia mano
a sfiorare le macchie rapprese
sul pavimento dell'altare.

Per trasmissione
                    sono sicuro
ne trarrai innumerevoli benefici
tu per prima
                    mia sorgiva segreta.

Mio pavido angelo della retroguardia.

The entrance barely visible
amid the debris and scaffolding
left in a tangle of neglect.
An olive grove discovered
because of your need to listen in
now crossed with hands clasped
your brisk steps of a confidante
headed for the miraculous small vault.

Wearing pearls the colour of lipstick
you pardon yourself – out of respect
for this sacred place – joining
my hand instead
to scarcely touch the stains
on the altar steps.

From this
                    I'm sure
you'll receive countless graces
you, first of all
                                my secret source.

My frightened angel guarding the rear.

Alla funzione domenicale
gli piaceva cadenzare con vigore
il turibolo per poi aspirarne
profondamente l'incenso
fin quasi allo stordimento.

Fu trovato una sera d'inverno
sul greto del fiume
prono
con i capelli che lambivano l'acqua.

In paese lo ricordano anche
come quello che cercava la luna
attraverso le grate dei cancelli.

At Sunday Mass, he liked to
swing the censer vigorously
inhaling deeply
till he was almost overcome.

He was found one evening
in winter, stretched out on the bank
of the river
with his hair licking the water.

People thereabouts also remember
how he kept searching for the moon
through the iron grill of the gate.

Lugano 5:50

Nell'angolo della funicolare che all'alba
mi trasporta alla stazione mentre
il cielo deve ancora liberare la sua luce
scarto rapidamente dal sonno al disagio
per l'uomo seduto dirimpetto
che mi fissa con insolente insistenza.
Immobile e venefico (uno di quei tipi
– diresti – che non sai mai cosa nascondono
in tasca e dietro gli occhi) non smette
di scrutarmi per tutto il tempo della risalita
con quel mezzo sorriso beffardo che spalanca
botole sotto i miei piedi.

Poi finalmente l'attracco
                                  la liberazione
dello sportello aperto sui box della biglietteria.
Lui non accenna a muoversi: aspetta che io
per primo mi guadagni l'uscita.
Nel guizzo che colgo oltrepassandolo
è chiaro il godimento
la soddisfazione di uno che ha verificato
ancora una volta la consistenza
del colpo in canna.

Lugano 5:50

In the corner of the funicular
taking me to the station at dawn
while the sky has yet to release its light
I quickly resist an uneasy sleep
because of the persistent, insolent stare
from the man sitting opposite.
Completely still and venomous (one of those types
– I can tell you – where you never know what's
hidden in his pocket or behind his eyes) he doesn't
stop scrutinizing me for the entire ascent
with that half-mocking smile
that throws a trapdoor wide open
under my feet.

Then finally we dock –
                                        the freedom
of a counter open for tickets.
He makes no sign of a move: he expects me
to be first to reach the exit.
His pleasure is obvious
in the flicker I catch going past him
the satisfaction of having proven, once again
the persistence of the blow
with a cane.

Nella tua mente rimasta fanciulla
c'è un'ombra
              sempre lei
                         così vicina.

In your mind a child remains
a shade
            always
                    so close.

Non conoscevano loro
il passo della fuga
l'equilibrio oscillante
sopra la slitta azzurra.

È stato dopo un'abbondante nevicata
durata tutta la notte
che è giunta l'ora quieta
esatta
           del loro addio.

They didn't know
of the path of the flight
the wavering pulse
on its blue glide downward.

It was after an abundant snowfall
lasting all night
that the stillness came
the instant
             of their farewell.

Proteggimi
        isola mia
e fa che la terra comune
non si spacchi in due
portandoti via.
Io ti trattengo dalla mia sponda
con mani tremanti e ti sento
scivolare lenta
           lenta.
Sarò nell' acqua per trattenerti
e conservare il più a lungo possibile
il tuo respiro nel mio.

Purché non ti rassegni
ad abbandonare la presa
inabissandoti esausta.

Purché in te viva il desiderio
di rimanere con me
dalla parte del giorno.

Protect me
        my island
and make sure that the land we share
does not split in two
carrying you away.
With trembling hands I hold you back
from the shore and feel you
slipping slowly
           slowly.
I will enter the water to hold you here
and for as long as possible
keep your breath in mine.

Provided you do not give up
and in letting go
sink exhausted.

Provided the desire to stay with me
lives on, joined by
the light of day.

– Non partirò. Non andrò
in nessun luogo se non vorrai –
sussurra dal finestrino del treno
in sosta mentre con un guizzo
controlla l'ora e il sorriso
le si increspa per il cielo basso
che in lontananza promette pioggia.

Vattene allora
                    mia Colchide.
Vai pure lontano
a diffondere altrove il tuo veleno.

– I won't leave. I won't go anywhere
if you don't want me to –
her murmurings from the window
of the waiting train
and squirming as she checks the time
her smile turns into a pout
at the sight of distant heavy skies
that promise rain.

Then go
          my Medea.
Just go away
and spread your poison elsewhere.

La tarda estate entra nella stanza
da tre finestre spalancate.
Tavolo e libri ne assumono lentamente
il colore dorato.

«Non avresti dovuto
per questo
distoglierti dal lavoro (stanare
aggettivi e verbi da far confluire
nell'armonicità della frase detta
ad alta voce): così allentata
la mente ridiviene facile preda
dell'oscuro pulpito della memoria».

Nella stanza al terzo piano
ora
può aver luogo il carosello delle voci.

Late summer enters the room
with its three windows thrown open.
Table and books slowly assume
the colour of gold.

               "This
                         shouldn't have disturbed
                your work (the drawing out
                of verbs and adjectives, turning
                them into harmoniously flowing
                phrases spoken aloud): a mind so
                relaxed easily falls prey once again
                to the darkened stage of memory."

Now
          the whirl of voices can take place
in the third floor room.

Per la tua troppo innocente esistenza
mi scopro di tanto in tanto a pensarti
come ad un angelo senza palpebre
rivolto verso il sole.

It is your too-innocent life which
now and then leaves me thinking about you
like an angel, wide-eyed, turned
towards the sun.

È sempre stata la mia persecuzione
quell'attendere immobile
                              al bivio
la cadenza delle tue mutazioni:
lo sguardo lungamente stretto
(io dov'ero?)
sugli sfilacci della tovaglia azzurra
le improvvise ire
e le altrettanto rapide capitolazioni
in cui riuscivi perfino giocosa
modulando la tua voce
                              per ore
come quella di una bambina.

Col tempo
            per soffrirne meno
ho imparato ogni volta a ripiegare
schivando quanti più colpi possibili.
A disinfettarmi le ferite
soltanto con la saliva.

My torment always
was to wait motionless
                              at the crossroads
for the tone of your changing moods:
that slowly narrowing stare
(where was I?)
the sudden anger
over some disorder of the blue tablecloth
the equally rapid giving way
when, playfully, you even managed
to change your voice
                              for long spells
to that of a little child's.

Gradually
            I learned to suffer less
by retreating each time –
dodging as many blows as possible.

            And
by licking them
to disinfect my wounds.

Anima corallii

Incide il tuo collo
come ruggine altera
come emorragia di una ferita
la vampa recisa che stilla
nell'inudibile alfabeto
la sua frantumata sembianza
di sangue coagulato del mare.

Anima Corallii

Etched on your neck
like rust's erosion
like an unstaunched wound,
by a resolute flame distilling
in silent letters
its shattered semblance
of the sea's blood congealed.

Lasciati trasportare dal fiume ombroso
senza timore
               Ruth dei Moabiti.
Affida il tuo dolce carro al centro
della corrente e non guardare
il branco di lupe che lo costeggiano
dalle sponde.

Trenta uccelli notturni vegliano
perché tu possa prendere riva
incolume a nord di Sadagora.
Là
     tra le spighe più alte
ti attende Paolo: fuggite insieme
senza voltarvi a guardare lo scintillio
dei canini in avvicinamento.

Presto lo saprete entrambi che alla fine
saranno comunque loro
                    ad avere il sopravvento.

Let yourself be carried by the shaded river
without fear
              Ruth of the Moabites.
Entrust your gentle burden to the centre
of the current and disregard
the pack of she-wolves running on the banks
alongside.

Thirty nocturnal birds keep watch
so that you can safely reach the shore
north of Sadagora.
There
        among the taller reeds
Paul waits for you: escape together
without turning round to see the glint
of bared teeth coming closer.

Soon you'll both know
in the end
              they will prevail.

In ciascun giorno della mia voce
da ora
          che gli spasmi dell'attesa
si sono purificati nella luce sobria
di una nuova sicumera
e il miele dell'autunno
si è infine addensato sulla
sua spiga
          posso dire: sì
sono stata io la sposa del vento.

With my voice, each day
from the moment
                    the agony of waiting
has been refined in the sober light
of a new vainglory
and autumn's honey
has thickened at last
on the grain
            I can say: yes *I*
was the bride of the wind.

«I gabbiani del Tevere
non scordano mai
i lanciatori di sassi».

E quante volte anche tu
                   Elio
attraversando i miasmi di Roma
dopo aver soggiaciuto agli sfoghi
infantili di tanti padri Tiresia
hai giurato di non prestare più
a nessuno la tua voce
per tentare finalmente da solo
la vertigine del volo.

Eppure
         il ricordo filtrato
dalla garza del tempo ti porta ora
con sempre maggiore frequenza
a invertire le vesti e a interpretare
con la stessa dolenza
perfino con la medesima voce strascicata
quel ruolo di esegeta
che avevi ripudiato.

«Con gli anni diventiamo tutti
ciò che avevamo temuto»

giustifichi me per te stesso
mentre il riflesso già investe
anche la spiaggia di sabbia tiepida
e pietre aguzze da cui sei partito.

"No Tiber seagull
ever forgets
the stone-throwers."

And how many times
                    have you, Elio
in your wanderings through Rome's
miasmas – after being the subject
of infantile attacks
from so many Tiresian fathers –
vowed never to lend your voice again
to anyone, in an attempt
to fly the vertiginous heights alone.

However
            now, with the siftings
of memory, you are brought
to a complete reversal – you interpret
with the same despair – you even
adopt the same drawl as all
those hierophants
you once repudiated.

"With the passing of years
we become like those we've dreaded."

And with that you vindicate us both
while reflections strike the beach's
lukewarm sand and the sharp stones
you've left behind.

(Nel sonno
                    qualche volta
ti ascolto invocare i gorghi
del mare Adriatico:
ognuno di loro ha il nome
di uno dei poeti che hai narrato.
Il sussulto che ti sveglia
caduto tra i fantasmi
è l'ultimo diaframma che separa
la tua dalla loro vita).

(Sometimes
            in sleep
I hear you cry out
to the whirlpools of the Adriatic:
each with the name
of a poet you used to quote.
The tremor that wakes you
as it crashes among these ghosts
is the last barrier
separating your life from theirs.)

Notes

Preface: Mario Luzi's citation is from Tiziano Broggiato, *Predizione dell'albero secco*, Udine, Italy: Campanotto, 1991, p. 7.

"No Tiber seagull ..." is dedicated to Elio Pecora.

"Umbra Sine Spe" and "Window of a Skyscraper," both previously published, have been revised for inclusion in this almost complete selection from *Parca lux*.

Acknowledgements

Translations appeared in the following publications:

Stand, Volume 6(4) & 7(1): "Celan's Affliction"

Gradiva, Number 30, Fall 2006: "Umbra Sine Spe" and "Window of a Skyscraper"

Atlanta Review, Spring/Summer 2011: "Return to Peschiera del Garda" and "The entrance barely visible"

The translators wish to express their deepest appreciation to Peter Davidson, who has given generously of his time to read and comment on the translations at various levels of completion. The final responsibility, however, rests entirely with the translators.

About the Author/ Translators

Tiziano Broggiato was born in Vicenza in 1953, where he currently lives. Among his most recent publications are: *Dieci poesie* (Almanacco dello Specchio n°3, Mondadori, Milano, 2007), *Anticipo della notte* (Marietti, Milano, 2006), *Parca lux* (Marsilio, Venezia, 2001) which was awarded the prestigious Premio Montale and the Premio dell'Unione Lettori Italiani. He also edited two anthologies, *Canti dall'universo – Dodici poeti italiani degli anni ottanta* (Marcos y Marcos, Milano, 1988) and *Lune gemelle* (Palomar, Bari, 1998). His poetry has been translated into several languages: Spanish, French, English, Croatian, Serbian and Greek. Broggiato's latest collection of poems entitled *Città alla fine del mondo* will be published by Laca Book (Milan) in 2013.

Toronto poet and musician Patricia Hanley not only taught the recorder and viola da gamba, but performed in various ensembles. Her poetry has been published in literary journals in Canada, U.S.A., and South Africa and, in translation, in Italy. More recently, she translated her own poems into Italian, eight of which were shortlisted for the Italian prize, "Premio Colline di Torino, 2011." A bilingual edition of her poems, *Sotto la scrittura corsiva*, was published in Italy in 2012 (ellerani editore).

Born in Rome and presently living in Toronto, Maria Laura Mosco holds a 'Laurea' in Modern Languages from the University of Rome La Sapienza with a post graduate specialization in Literary Translation. From the University of Toronto she holds a Master of Arts in Italian Studies and Semiotics. She has long standing experience as a literary and technical translator. Her research interests range from Italian Literature and Cinema to Theory of Translation and Language Pedagogy.